T0163577

An Embarrassment *of* Misprints

Comical and Disastrous Typos of the Centuries

Max Hall

Fulcrum Publishing
Golden, Colorado

Cover design by Alyssa Pumphrey

Library of Congress Cataloging-in-Publication Data
Hall, Max.
    An embarrassment of misprints / Max Hall.
       p.   cm.
    Includes bibliographical references (p.) and index.
    ISBN 1-55591-202-8
    1. Errata. I. Title.
Z242.E77H35   1995
686.2'25–dc20   95-19646
                                 CIP

Printed in the United States of America

0 9 8 7 6 5 4 3 2 1

Fulcrum Publishing
350 Indiana Street, Suite 350
Golden, Colorado 80401-5093
800/992-2908

Contents

Preface

Some people are bird watchers. I am a typo watcher. I have been intrigued by typographical errors nearly all my life. As a newspaper person, Washington information officer, book editor, and teacher of writing—and simply as a reader—I have seen plenty of mix-ups.

Even as a schoolboy in Atlanta, Georgia, I made a note of an error that appeared on April 24, 1925, in the *O'Keefe Log,* our school paper at O'Keefe Junior High. The paper mentioned "a very disappointing showing of our track coach, Mr. Townsend." A week later came a correction. The story as written had said the team had made "a very disappointing showing after such untiring efforts on the part of our track coach, Mr. Townsend." Thus at an early age I learned that typos can damage reputations.

About thirty-five years later, in January 1961, I published my first article about typos. It came out in *Nieman Reports,* a journalism quarterly, under the title "Printers' Errors, Ancient and Modern, and Not Always Accidental."

Thirty-two more years passed and my pile of typos grew larger. I put some of them in a longer article for *Harvard Magazine's* July–August 1993 issue and called it "An Embarrassment of Misprints." (Despite strenuous proofreading, a pesky little error showed up in that article.) Readers sent in their favorite typos, and the magazine printed many of them in the next few issues. The article itself was reprinted in three other periodicals.

All this encouraged me to expand that article into a book having the same title.

In doing so, I thank those who contributed interesting typos. When using their offerings, I mention their names either in the text or in the Notes and Credits section at the back of the book. The participation of so many people makes this book a congenial cooperative enterprise.

I also thank *Harvard Magazine,* especially the managing editor, Christopher Reed, who is helpfully involved in every book I write.

And I thank my offspring, Clay, Nancy, and Judy, for helping me make the manuscript a lot better than it would have been.

Max Hall
April 1995

An Invitation From the Author

Readers who know of highly interesting misprints that are not found in this book are invited to send them to me for use in a possible sequel. I can't promise to publish them, but at least you'll have one very appreciative reader. Tell me, if you can, just where and when those colossal bloopers occurred; send a clipping or photocopy if possible. Please address them to me in care of Fulcrum Publishing, 350 Indiana Street, Suite 350, Golden, CO 80401-5093.

Chapter 1

A Somewhat Unscientific Typology of Typ°s

"Printers have persecuted me without a cause." That anguished cry appears in the 119th Psalm, verse 161, in a Bible published around 1702. Actually the persecutors were "princes," not "printers." The edition with the misprint has been called the "Printers' Bible."

Though the author was not present to groan over that error, a good many other authors during the last five centuries have indeed felt persecuted by printers.

Granted, most of the misinformation published since the time of Gutenberg has been the fault of writers and editors. Typographical errors are less worrisome—typos that survive the proofreading process are usually trivial and merely messy, and not worth remembering.

Nevertheless, some of the misprints over the centuries do invite our attention because they are entertaining, or because they altered meanings and deceived readers. Those memorable misprints are the subject of this book. My aim is not only to quote them but to sort them into categories, like plants or animals.

My definition of a misprint is "an alteration during the process of getting something into print that makes it different from what it was supposed to say." This is broad enough to cover not only the actions of typesetters but also deviations of other kinds, such as the dropping of words or lines after the type has been set. It also includes *deliberate* alterations during the printing process if they changed the author's meaning.

Misprints (typos), when collected in large numbers, can be observed to fall into groups:

- ☞ Some of the most insidious typos happen through omission of the word "not."
- ☞ Some misprints are perpetrated out of mischief or malice.
- ☞ Some consist of the unlucky insertion of things that were not meant to be printed.
- ☞ Some result from the peculiar vulnerability of certain words.
- ☞ Misprints occur not only in words but also in numbers, such as dates, people's ages, and dollar amounts, and these wrong numbers can be funny or distressing.
- ☞ Some misprints occur in the process of correcting other misprints.
- ☞ Some can be blamed on atrocious handwriting.
- ☞ Some have been blamed on the Devil.

Misprints of all kinds, when judged by their effects, can be classified as either (1) only amusing, or (2) only hurtful, or (3) both. The misprints that are both amusing and hurtful can be especially intriguing. The misprints that interest me the most are those that aren't detectable as misprints. That is, we as readers do not know that we are getting wrong information.

I shall give examples of all these types of typos and more, though not exactly in that order. The groups overlap a lot, so a particular misprint is apt to fall into more than one group. To illustrate: The dropping of "not" from one of the Ten Commandments (yes, it happened) would fit into the chapter called Ouch! Misleading and Hurtful or the chapter called Calamitous Omissions, but I have chosen to place it in the chapter called Accidental or Deliberate?

Many of my examples were committed when printing was done with metal and the typesetting was done by hand, letter by letter, or by Linotype machines, which produced solid metal lines. Many other misprints in my collection happened in recent decades, when computers have taken over and metal type has just about melted into history. Typesetting nowadays is performed by someone sitting at a computer keyboard and tapping out a text which is captured on a disk in the machine, and then generated electronically in a form that can be used in offset printing. The keyboarding is done not only by professional typesetters but by other people, including editors and authors.

An interesting question arises: Which method produced more typographical errors, the old or the new? I don't know the answer. Reasonable arguments can be made on both sides. Some people think the old system produced more typos because metal letters or lines were physical objects that could be dropped or put in the wrong place in a composing room through no fault of the typesetter. But others think the new system produces more typos because a lot of amateurs are setting type and there are fewer professional proofreaders.

One thing we can be sure of: High tech has not eradicated misprints.

Newspapers actually suffered a big increase in typos during the 1960s and 1970s, when they were adopting the new methods and eliminating the jobs of many traditional typesetters. Even after the technology was in operation, there were "bugs" in the computer programming. But the bugs were largely overcome, and human sloppiness recovered its rightful place as chief culprit.

Chapter 2

Bloopers That Only Tickle

Here are some typos that were entertaining but not seriously misinforming. They probably embarrassed those who were responsible for them, but they didn't inflict damage on the public. In fact, the public may have been pleased to have its day brightened a little.

In the spring of 1990 the U. S. Naval Academy presented 990 diplomas to its graduating class with "Naval" spelled "Navel." A representative of the Academy told me the flawed documents arrived from the printer the day before the ceremony, and there was nothing to do but hand them out. A corrected version was later sent to each graduate.

"Naval," it seems, is one of those "vulnerable words" that will be discussed in a later chapter. On December 3, 1993, the *Manchester Cricket,* in Manchester, Massachusetts, said that the author of a new maritime book "is known as the master of the navel confrontational novel." John Bethell, at that time the editor of *Harvard Magazine,* who lives in Manchester, suggested that this item could be entitled "Belly to Belly in the South Pacific."

The *New York Times* of August 20, 1962, printed a dinner menu said to be reasonable in cost. The first course was given as "consommé with poodles." (This was corrected to "noodles" in the Late City Edition.)

According to a story that has made the rounds for at least seventy years, a book printed at the Riverside Press contained extravagant praise of that company's proofreading—but unfortunately the word came out "poofreading." Three well-known publishers, Edward Weeks, F. N. Doubleday, and Ferris Greenslet, mentioned this error in their memoirs, but they gave three different versions of where it occurred, and I cannot find it in the books they named.

In January 1971 the Bicentennial Commission in Washington, D.C., sent out a newsletter referring to the approaching "200th anniversary of the Untied States."

An unintentional report of a fatality appeared in one of my writings when I was in the Washington bureau of the Associated Press. In a Sunday feature for February 25, 1951, I wrote that Michael V. DiSalle, the Director of Price Stabilization, popped out of a plane in Toledo and "kissed his wife, Myrtle." One of the papers that printed the story, the *News and Courier* in Charleston, South Carolina, had me saying that he "killed his wife, Myrtle." (Startled readers could tell from the story that no slaying had taken place.)

When Harvard University Press gave an award to Professor Evon Z. Vogt, a native of New Mexico, the *Gallup Independent* on June 22, 1970, headed the story thus:

EVEN VOGT IS AWARDED
HARVARD FACULTY PRIZE

According to a history of the *Washington Post*, that paper once printed this headline on the front page of its first edition:

FDR IN BED
WITH COED

Actually President Roosevelt was in bed with a cold, as the story made clear. Chalmers Roberts, author of the history, wrote that this misprint probably occurred in 1940, and that the President phoned the paper and ordered a hundred copies to send to his friends. But Roosevelt didn't get his copies, said Roberts, because the circulation department had scurried around to retrieve the edition and shred it.

The headline about President Roosevelt brings to mind one of the best-known typos of all, the eight-column headline about a governor who signed a lot of bills at the close of a legislative session. What it said was:

GOVERNOR'S PEN IS BUSY OVER WEEKEND

At least it was supposed to look like that, but the line was so tight there was hardly any space between the words, so that it looked more like this:

GOVERNOR'SPENISBUSYOVERWEEKEND

I think I saw that headline a long time ago but it never was in my possession and I must admit I don't have the clipping now.

Numbers, like words, are sometimes misstated by typesetters. Here are a few wrong numbers from the *New York Times*'s early edition delivered to homes in New England. Their dates are in the Notes and Credits section at the back of this book.

A 5-year-old former Meridian truck driver was a murder suspect in Mississippi.

Luci Baines Johnson, daughter of President Johnson, converted to Catholicism on July 3, 1965, but her date of birth was given as July 2, 1967.

During a murder trial in Selma, Alabama, a television repairman, 3 years old, was called to the stand.

Many of the bloopers in my collection are from the *Times*, but this only means that I was reading the *Times* more carefully than other newspapers. Those three errors occurred in

1965, during the upheaval in printing technology. But of course all decades produce misprinted numbers. Twelve years later, when a movie was being made in Brooklyn, a 181-year-old stunt man was hired as an extra, according to the *Times*.

And even more recently, in 1991, the *Boston Globe* said the composer Tchaikovsky conducted a concert at Carnegie Hall on May 5, 1981. On that date the composer had been dead for eighty-eight years.

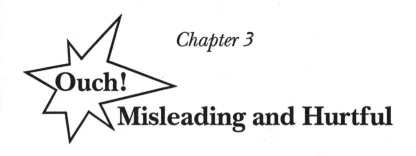

Chapter 3

Ouch!
Misleading and Hurtful

The *Washington Post* headline "FDR IN BED WITH COED" did not ruin President Roosevelt, but a later typo dragged the same paper into court.

In 1976 three youths were being tried for a shooting on a bus. A story in the *Post* said that Michael Donaldson had "pleaded guilty to second degree murder." He had really pleaded "not guilty." The *Post* printed a correction and said the "not" had been dropped inadvertently. Donaldson was acquitted of the murder charge, whereupon he sued the paper for libel. The court ruled against him on the grounds that the case had made him a public figure and that the misprint was not malicious.

The next typographical error in the "hurtful" category is one about the Archbishop of Canterbury that is comical to typo watchers but perhaps not to the Archbishop. On January 18, 1961, the International Edition of the *New York Times*, published in London, referred to him as "the red-nosed Archbishop" (meaning "red-robed").

Some of the most interesting mistakes in newspapers happen when headlines attach themselves to the wrong stories. When two headlines somehow swap places, the result can be confusing, hilarious, or horrifying. Grady Clay, a journalist in Louisville, Kentucky, sent me a fine specimen. Here is his description of a headline switch of more than fifty years ago in *The Record*, a newspaper in Troy, New York:

> During World War II when the paper was short-staffed, two important events happened the same day: a historic ice-house on the banks of the Hudson River burned to the ground; and a most prominent local social figure, the wife of a well-known businessman, died. Unfortunately, the headline over the lady's picture belonged over the picture of the ice-house. It read: **"OLD EYESORE GONE AT LAST."**

I include "Old Eyesore" in my "hurtful" chapter because, though we laugh at it now, it presumably was not a laughing matter to the deceased woman's loved ones. This item, by the way, illustrates the difficulty of documenting typos that live in people's memories. Grady Clay had heard the "Old Eyesore" story from Dwight Marvin, a long-ago editor and publisher of the Troy newspaper. I asked Clay if he could provide the date of the mix-up. He queried the newspaper and was told that retrieval at this late date was next to impossible.

Eliot B. Spalding, who was editor of the *Cambridge Chronicle* for about thirty years, wrote to tell me of two misprints that rival the Case of the Old Eyesore. He caught them in proof, "thanks be to God," as he said. Here they are, in Spalding's words:

1. A caption under the front-page picture of a prominent society woman was supposed to read "Heads Monthly Flower Show," but the printer omitted two letters, making it "Heads Monthly Flow Show."
2. In a headline saying that a well-known couple had announced the engagement of their daughter, the word "engagement" came out "enlargement."

"Consommé with poodles," mentioned earlier, probably didn't mislead anybody, but errors in recipes can cause inconvenience and even physical pain. In 1991 the *New York Times* related some of those gastronomical mishaps in a feature article. For example, a recent *Times* recipe had called for one-fourth cup of pepper (instead of one-fourth teaspoon), and there was a terrible scene in a Florida household when the family dug into chicken prepared according to the misprint.

Gremlins vs. Scholars

Many a scholar has taken a wrong turn, thereby suffering professional injury, because of a typographical error. Herman Melville's *White-Jacket*, first published in 1850, provides a classic case.

Near the end of the novel, an account of a sailor's fall from a yardarm into the water includes this passage: "But of a sudden some fashionless form brushed my side—some inert, coiled fish of the sea." In the early 1920s, when the Standard Edition of Melville's works was published in London, a printer hit a wrong key and "coiled fish" became "soiled fish."

F. O. Matthiessen of Harvard analyzed this passage in his 1941 book *American Renaissance*. Unaware that "soiled" was a misprint, he said it was "a twist of imagery of the sort that was to become peculiarly Melville's." He declared that "hardly anyone but Melville could have created the shudder that results from calling this frightening vagueness some '*soiled* fish of the sea.'"

A typo with a far more discombobulating impact on the world of scholarship may have occurred in 1609 when the sublime sonnets generally attributed to William Shakespeare were first published.

The poems were preceded by an epigraph wishing all happiness to a certain "Mr. W. H.," described as "the onlie begetter" of the sonnets. This epigraph became one of the most chewed-over puzzles in all literature. Who was Master W. H., and what was his relationship to Shakespeare? Over the centuries various theories were advanced.

In 1987, Donald Foster of Vassar College argued that W. H. was Shakespeare himself, and that the initial had probably been written as "W. S." or "W. SH." by the publisher and fouled up by a typesetter. As long ago as the 1860s the possibility of a misprint had been suggested and laughed at. Professor Foster, in a very detailed article, made a strong case that the misprint hypothesis fits the known facts better than any other.

A misprint in an examination question once had an interesting effect on a young student of colonial history. The professor who gave the exam was Richard H. Shryock, of Philadelphia. He asked his students to discuss the "New Jersey grants." Whoever typed the exam sheet hit a wrong key and made it "New Jersey giants." Shryock spotted the error and notified the class. Everybody had a good laugh. One student, however, came in late, failed to get the correction, and proceeded to write several pages on the New Jersey giants, describing them as a race of tall, blond, Stone Age people who inhabited the hills and valleys of New Jersey before the Europeans arrived.

I myself was a victim of a misprint in my copy of Addison and Steele's *The Spectator*. In an essay on March 13, 1711, Richard Steele gave his version of a sensational story about an Englishman who was saved from death by an Indian maiden and showed his gratitude by selling her into slavery. I was investigating this affair in 1953. In the edition I owned, published in 1843, Steele cited his source as "Lignon's Account of Barbadoes." During the next fifteen months I wasted a good deal of time searching for that source, and I decided that Lignon and his book must have been fabricated by Steele. Then, in another edition of *The Spectator*, I happened to notice that the name was Ligon, not Lignon, after which everything fell into place.

Such incidents teach a sad lesson. We cannot trust the accuracy of what we see in print. Even if the author was correct, the typesetter may not have been.

Wrong words can injure not only individuals but also institutions. In 1987 a highly praised book, *American Gardens of the Nineteenth Century*, by Ann Leighton, contained a bewildering mistake that sorely grieved the folks at the Massachusetts Historical Society. That society, founded in 1791, has a magnificent research library, which continues to grow from decade to decade. Yet the book on American gardens said that "the diminution of the fabulous Massachusetts Historical Society Library, with the sale of its treasures and the boxing up of its working historical references, was a great loss."

Astounded at this, Louis L. Tucker, director of the historical society, wrote to the publisher of the book, the University of Massachusetts Press. The press's director, Bruce Wilcox, as surprised as anybody, apologized and ordered a correction for the next printing. The correction was made. The passage should have said "Massachusetts Horticultural Society Library," but somehow "Horticultural" had been changed to "Historical."

That episode illustrates how hard it is, sometimes, to assign the blame for errors. No one seems to know how the word "Historical" got into the sentence. It could have been a printer's error, but it doesn't really look like one. More likely, the author or someone else had a little spell of absentmindedness. Maybe it was a "Freudian slip," or perhaps poor handwriting was involved (topics to be discussed in Chapter 6). The author, Isadora Smith, who wrote under the name Ann Leighton, was terminally ill at the time. She turned in a huge manuscript and had little part in the long process of rewriting and editing.

Many other errors of the past offer no clue as to whether the culprit was the author, editor, or printer. For example, I remember noticing that the title "Dogood Papers" (a series of youthful writings by Benjamin Franklin) was rendered in the *Harvard Crimson* as "Dogwood Papers." Who is to say, decades later, whether this blunder was made by the reporter, the editor, or the typesetter?

When Ruth Bader Ginsburg was called "Mr. Ginsburg" beneath her photograph in the Harvard Law School yearbook of 1972, was it a printer who omitted the *"s"* in "Mrs."? Maybe so, but one can't be sure. (Mrs. Ginsburg was then a visiting lecturer at Harvard, one day each week. This was twenty-one years before she was appointed to the U.S. Supreme Court.)

Consider the case of Charles E. Zemko, who wrote to a Connecticut newspaper, the *Regional Standard,* during a political campaign in 1993. In his letter as printed, he referred to the town employees of Salem, Connecticut, in this way: "The workers' morals would not be so low if they were allowed to do something useful and be properly recognized for it."

Without other evidence I would have strongly suspected that "morals" was a mistake and that a typesetter had done the deed. But, after a Salem selectman demanded that Zemko apologize to the town employees, the paper quoted Zemko as saying he had meant to write "morale" but had mistakenly left off the "e." This seemed to be confirmed by the fact that he had sent substantially the same communication to the *Norwich Bulletin,* where the controversial word had appeared in the singular—"moral." This doesn't tell us who supplied the "s" in the *Regional Standard,* making it "morals." Perhaps I will find out some day.

"Moral," "morality," and related words have popped up more than once in my typo watching.

In that connection, here is an instructive case of a disaster averted by alert proofreading. My friend Peggy Lamson's book entitled *Speaking of Galbraith* came out in 1991. In a passage on John Kenneth Galbraith's childhood in Canada, she told how the death of his mother had devastated the family, and concerning Galbraith's father she wrote: "Nor would he permit his many relatives to step in and try to help him bring back some sense of normality into their lives." After the manuscript was set in type, the author, reading proof, had a shock. Through a printer's error the words "bring back some sense of normality" had become "bring back some sense of morality." This typo, unlike the ones described above, was corrected before publication, but think of the consternation if it hadn't been.

Another such error was committed by the printers of the *Journal of Health and Social Behavior,* and it wasn't caught in proof. An article entitled "Gender and Health" began in some confusion with a reference to "recent trends in health and morality." But the article was not about morals. The phrase should have been "health and mortality."

In 1990 the Public Broadcasting System was the victim of a similar misprint on the package containing *Journey to America,* one of its videotapes for sale. This time "immorality" was the word that was supposed to be printed. Instead the sentence came out like this: "An immigrant could be rejected for any of a dozen reasons—communicable disease, illiteracy, no visible means of support or the very suspicion of immortality."

Losing the Numbers Game

The preceding chapter contained some erroneous numbers that were so ridiculous nobody could take them seriously. But many erroneous numbers are not so easily recognized as false. Here is a sampling from the *New York Times* and the *Boston Globe*, the principal papers I was reading at the time of the errors. The stories say:

- ☞ That the slabs at Stonehenge had heretofore been dated to about 170 B.C. This was a misprint for 1700 B.C.
- ☞ That the new national standard for sulphur oxides in the atmosphere was 0.80 micrograms per cubic meter. The correct figure was 80, not 0.80, but the wrong number ran on page one in all editions. It was corrected the next day and blamed on a transmission error.
- ☞ That the annual growth rate in world energy was 1.7 percent. This was a misprint for 5.7 percent. It was corrected six days later.
- ☞ That the builder of a new incinerator in Saugus, Massachusetts, told communities he would charge them $1 per ton to burn their garbage. This was good news for the communities, but alas, $1 was a misprint for $13.
- ☞ That the governor of Massachusetts had granted $36 billion to cities and towns. Again, a bonanza for the communities! But $36 billion was a misprint for $36 *million*.

The most consequential dollar error that has come to my attention was not committed by a newspaper. It was an error by a typist in a New York law firm who was pounding out a mortgage agreement in 1986. All she did was omit three zeros from the figure $92,885,000. The story was told by David Margolick in his column headed "At the Bar" in the *New York Times* of October 4, 1991. The figure in question was supposed to be what United States Lines owed the Prudential Insurance Company. According to

Margolick, the mistake was "overlooked by numerous supposedly crackerjack lawyers at several New York law firms, has generated a spate of litigation, hundreds of thousands of dollars in legal fees, millions of dollars in damages and an untold fortune in embarrassment."

Even a much more modest garbling of a number can inflict mortification. I know this from personal experience. Writing a booklet for sale at Harvard's Museum of Comparative Zoology, I quoted an eminent ornithologist to the effect that the last capture of a Great Auk took place off the coast of Iceland in 1844. But the printer made it 1944, and I failed to catch it in proof. This may not sound like a huge disaster, but if you have ever been in the same boat you know it's uncomfortable. I had saddled the eminent ornithologist with an error of one hundred years. The eminent ornithologist himself pointed out the error.

If this book does nothing else, I hope it serves as a warning to those of you who are called upon to proof your own or someone else's writings. Look carefully at every word and number, and remember the Great Auk.

Some of the most misleading and damaging errata happen when words mysteriously disappear from a sentence and leave it saying something completely different. And that is the subject of the next chapter.

Chapter 4

Calamitous Omissions

Parts of sentences can be omitted in computer typesetting, but, as suggested in Chapter 1, this was more apt to happen during the centuries before computers were invented. Type then consisted of metal objects that were manipulated by hand and were bound, sometimes, to be dropped on the floor or put in the wrong place.

A line was dropped on the floor—or otherwise lost—in Woodstock, Vermont, on December 21, 1972. On that dark day the *Vermont Standard* declared, "Mr. Smith has been in Mary for the last week, let's all keep him in our thoughts and prayers." The reporter had written that Mr. Smith was in *Mary Hitchcock Memorial Hospital.* The eviscerated statement must have brought the central character some undeserved notoriety, which is why I have changed his name to Smith.

A misprint of the same kind occurred in 1960 while Yvonne de Gaulle was visiting New York City with her famous husband. The *New York Times* stated flatly that Madame de Gaulle "tries to avoid charitable works." There were no irregularities in the sentence to alert the reader to the presence of gremlins in the composing room. Two days later the paper explained that a line of type had been accidentally omitted, and that the original sentence had said she *tries to avoid publicity but is active in charitable works.* But in libraries all over the world the faulty statement lives on in microfilm, lying in ambush for some researcher who will use the *Times* as trustingly as if it were a dictionary.

On another occasion, in 1962, the dropping of eleven words from the *Times* (probably two lines of metal type) had a labor leader saying the opposite of what he really said. Again the erroneous passage read smoothly, showing no gremlin fingerprints. Joseph Curran, president of the National Maritime Union, had sent a telegram to George Meany, president of the AFL-CIO, about possible raids against the maritime union's membership. The newspaper quoted one part of the telegram as follows: "We are not concerned about what such activity can do to the labor movement." Eight days later it printed a letter from Curran protesting that his telegram had actually said, "We are not concerned about anything that can be done to us. We are concerned about what such activity can do to the labor movement."

In 1969 the omission of only one word made a big difference in a *Times* story. A settlement was announced under which $120 million would be refunded to consumers who had alleged they were overcharged for certain antibiotics. The news story told what a consumer had to do to get a refund. For one thing, the consumer must "state he was reimbursed by someone else—such as a health insurance plan—for the purchase." In the Late City Edition the missing word was restored. It was "whether." The sentence was supposed to say the consumer must also state *whether* he was reimbursed.

In 1972 another omission of a single word harmed a former U.S. Surgeon General, Dr. Luther L. Terry. The *Times,* in reporting that he called for the abolishment of all tobacco advertising, called him (in the early editions) "a smoker." By the final edition this had been corrected to "a former smoker."

Still another omission, in 1973, harmed U.S. Senator Harold E. Hughes. The *Times* said he had initiated the bombing raids on Cambodia. According to a correction the next day, the sentence should have said that Senator Hughes initiated the *investigation* of the raids.

The appearance of those shockers in the distinguished *New York Times* leads one to believe that many other papers were fully as bad during that period of confusion in printing technology.

An omission of four words from the *Boston Globe* of July 27, 1972, had an explosive effect. In that day's paper a column by Ian Menzies began with this sentence: "The reputation and integrity of women recruited to work on the $3 1/2 million Boston Transportation Planning Review study is under serious challenge." This was not what Menzies had written. In the next day's paper he explained that he had actually begun this way: "The reputation and integrity of young professional men and women." The words "young professional men and" had vanished, leaving only "women" and causing Menzies (in his words) to be "nominated for the Male Chauvinist Pig award of the year by a large number of readers." He concluded, "With this explanation, I may now be able to return home."

Here are a couple of mortifying omissions from Harvard publications of some years ago:

A book entitled *An Introduction to Harvard* contained this passage: "On rare occasions the colonial government made special grants to the College, as when the General Court burned down Harvard Hall." Well, Harvard Hall did burn down—in 1764. The Massachusetts General Court helped rebuild it, but didn't light the fire. Obviously a few words went up in smoke.

A book published in 1954 contained messages from surviving members of the class of 1904. The message from Dr.

Edward Bell Krumbhaar, as printed, contained this sentence: "And here I might interject how different my choice of colleges might have been in the light of subsequent developments." He had really written "my choice of college courses," not "my choice of colleges," as he mournfully explained in a later report published by the class.

In 1948 the dropping of a line of type from the *Gainesville Times*, of Gainesville, Georgia, resulted in this surprising item:

8 P.M.: Nimocks–Overby Wedding First Methodist followed by bingo in the annex.

That was supposed to be two items, one on a prominent wedding and the other on an affair at the Legion Home. Sylvan Meyer, who was then editor of the Gainesville paper, has told me that the paper was young when the mix-up occurred, "and it dern near killed us for good."

Chapter 5

Embarr͟a͟ssing Insertions

The mistake about Madame de Gaulle's charitable works brings to mind an unconfirmed anecdote about Bret Harte (1836–1902). According to this yarn, Harte once wrote in his California newspaper that a resident named Mrs. Jones "has long been noted for her charity." The typesetter made it "has long been noted for her chastity." The proofreader put a question mark on the galley so that the typesetter would check the original copy. The item came out in the paper thus: "Mrs. Jones has long been noted for her chastity(?)."

Whether fact or fiction, that story illustrates a typographical genre consisting of things that got into print but were not supposed to.

An early example of such intrusions is found in a Bible printed at Cambridge, England, in 1805. The episode is described in *Brewer's Dictionary of Phrase & Fable*, which is my principal source on biblical eccentricities. The trouble arose in Galatians 4:29. The correct reading of this verse in the King James Version is: "But as then he that was born after the flesh persecuted him that was born after the Spirit, even so it is now." When this had been set in type the proofreader queried whether the comma after "Spirit" was correct. The editor answered by writing "to remain" in the margin of the galley proof. The typesetter inserted "to remain" after "Spirit," and that edition became known as the "To-remain Bible." Imagine a conscientious preacher of that time trying to figure out the meaning of "him that was born after the Spirit to remain."

Similarly, a century and a half later, an unwanted word wormed its way onto the cover of *Yankee* magazine. I have the story from Judson Hale, editor of that periodical. He recalled that in October 1960 the magazine printed a fiction story entitled "Sound of the Sea" and advertised it at the top of the front cover. The editors wanted to emphasize the word "Sound." In those days Hale (then an associate editor) made all changes in the cover by telephone. Over a somewhat faulty connection, he yelled to the printer, "Make 'Sound' big." So, instead of "SOUND of the Sea," the line came out "Sound Big of the Sea." In desperation the editors ordered that the printed cover be put back through the press so that the word "Big" could be overlaid with the silhouette of a bird. This was an ingenious remedy but not wholly successful: The bird wasn't quite dark enough to hide the extraneous word.

Printers once put some extraneous words at the beginning of an article by the astronomer Harlow Shapley, longtime director of the Harvard College Observatory. Joseph E. Dolan, of Laurel, Maryland, an astronomer himself, heard the story from Shapley in the 1960s, and in 1993 he wrote to me about it:

> Shapley had submitted a manuscript to the *Astrophysical Journal* that W. W. Campbell, the editor, had asked Edwin Hubble to review. Hubble's review, "Of no particular importance," was written in pencil on the title page of the manuscript when he returned it to Campbell. Campbell decided to publish the manuscript notwithstanding, and sent it to the printer. Luckily, Campbell caught the result in the galley proof stage before publication: the printer had set the byline in print as "by Harlow Shapley of no particular importance." Shapley said that Campbell kept the galley proof

in his desk drawer for years and took great delight in showing it to visiting astronomers (including Shapley!).

Dolan also said Shapley had problems getting people to spell his name correctly:

> When he made the cover of *Time*, even that worthy magazine misspelled his name once in the article as "Harlow Shapely." Three weeks after "his" cover had come out, Shapley appeared at an observatory staff meeting waving the current issue of *Time*, that week featuring a picture of Jean Harlow on the cover. "Look!" he said. "This week, the shapely Harlow; last time, Harlow Shapely."

In newspaper publishing, some extraneous words are built into the system. They are the editors' identifying tag lines, or "slugs," whose purpose is to ensure that every piece of copy will wind up in the right place. A story might be called **MURDER, FIRE, SENATE, ELECTION,** or **KOREA,** and those slugs are set in type along with the stories but are discarded when the pages are made up. When an existing story is augmented, the new piece of copy might be slugged **ADD MURDER, INSERT B FIRE, NEW LEAD ELECTION,** or whatever.

Slugs occasionally get in the paper by accident, so there is a well-known rule that they had better be printable. Once in the 1930s a printer on the *Athens Banner-Herald*, in Athens, Georgia, ignored the rule. I saw the result and can affirm under oath that it happened. The paper sponsored a cooking school and reported the event in a long story listing the women who attended. Column after column the list continued, and in the midst of it appeared this line:

ADD COOKING SCHOOL SHIT.

Chapter 6

Ac idental or Deliberate?

Newspaper offices are apt to harbor harrowing tales of famous typos. Around 1930, at the *Atlanta Constitution,* the first paper I worked on, I heard an anecdote that illustrates the category of misprints caused by poor handwriting. It went as follows. A long-ago *Constitution* editor scribbled this head-line late one night: "Land Grants in Hall" (meaning Hall County). It came out in the paper as "Loud Grunts in Hell."

If "Loud Grunts in Hell" was really set in type and printed in the newspaper, it may also belong in the category of mis-prints committed knowingly. Suppose the typesetter stared at the copy and said to the other printers, "Hey, look at this, loud grunts in hell." Everybody died laughing. Suppose too that the typesetter realized what the editor had meant but could not resist taking advantage of the situation. Printers, like other people, love a good joke. Some of the sensational misprints of the ages may have been printers' pranks. Thus, when a typo comes out *very funny,* a little skepticism may be in order. The Bible printer who set the line "Printers have persecuted me without a cause" may have known what he was doing.

Another biblical misprint, in 1631, is even more likely to have been deliberate. This error was so dreadful that the edi-tion in which it appeared became notorious as the "Wicked

Bible." The word "not" was omitted from the Seventh Commandment (Exodus 20:14), so that it commanded "Thou shalt commit adultery."

About eighty years after the "Wicked Bible," Joseph Addison wrote the following comment about it in *The Spectator* of August 11, 1714: "By the Practice of the World, which prevails in this degenerate Age, I am afraid that very many young Profligates, of both Sexes, are possessed of this spurious Edition of the Bible, and observe the Commandment according to that faulty Reading."

Fifteen years later, Benjamin Franklin, a printer well acquainted with Addison's writings—and with typographical errors—also mentioned the 1631 Bible, as will be discussed in the next chapter.

P. M. Handover, in her history of printing in London, says the "Wicked Bible" was called in and burnt, so that only a few copies have survived to modern times. She says too that the printing proprietor, Robert Barker, one of His Majesty's Printers, was ruined, and that it seems likely a rival printer, Bonham Norton, suborned the workmen to allow the blasphemous misprint to pass.

Further writes P. M. Handover:

> To realize how distressing it was for the injunction to appear as "Thou shalt commit adultery," it is necessary to imagine this page being read by someone earnest but relatively uneducated, whose Bible was perhaps the first book he had ever owned. How would he understand that a word had been left out? The seriousness of such a misprint cannot be exaggerated. Such an omission in a dictionary might lead to misunderstanding, but in a Bible it could imperil a man's immortal soul.

Even without imperiling a person's soul, such a mistake can be confusing. In all centuries there are those who take the Holy Scriptures literally as the word of God and know little about the very human activities of translators, editors, typesetters, and proofreaders. So the element of divine authority gives biblical misprints a special position.

Subverting Divine Authority

Brewer's Dictionary of Phrase & Fable offers a long list of Bibles that acquired nicknames in their day because of blunders. The "Printers' Bible," the "Wicked Bible," and the "To-remain Bible" have already been mentioned. Here are some others:

- ☞ Unrighteous Bible (1653). Paul's question "Know ye not that the unrighteous shall not inherit the Kingdom of God?" (1 Corinthians 6:9) was printed without the second "not," so that it read "Know ye not that the unrighteous shall inherit the Kingdom of God?"

- ☞ "Sin on" Bible (1716, said to be the first Bible printed in Ireland). "Sin no more" in John 5:14 appeared as "sin on more."

- ☞ Vinegar Bible (1717). "The parable of the vinegar" was a mistake for "The parable of the vineyard" in a heading above Luke 20. P. M. Handover says that the same edition, which was printed by John Baskett at Oxford, was also called the "Basketful of Errors."

- ☞ Murderers' Bible (1801). "Murderers" was a mistake for "murmurers" in Jude 1:16, a verse that ordinarily says "there are murmurers, complainers, walking after their own lusts."

- ☞ Lions Bible (1804). "Thy son that shall come forth out of thy loins" (1 Kings 8:19) was rendered "thy son that shall come forth out of thy lions."

The same 1804 edition contained another "murderer" misprint. "The murderer shall surely be put to death" (Numbers 35:18) was rendered "the murderer shall surely be put together."

Question: Which of those errors were accidental and which were printers' jokes? Who knows?

But, according to a strange story published in 1823, a woman in Germany made a biblical change that was certainly deliberate. Not liking what God said to Eve in the Garden of Eden, she took it upon herself to amend it. My source is a book by Isaac D'Israeli, father of Prime Minister Benjamin Disraeli, and he tells this story:

> A printer's widow in Germany, while a new edition of the Bible was printing at her house, one night took an opportunity of going into the office, to alter that sentence of subjection to her husband, pronounced upon Eve in Genesis, Chap. 3. v. 16. She took out the first two letters of the word HERR, and substituted NA in their place, thus altering the sentence from "and he shall be thy LORD" *(Herr)* to "and he shall be thy FOOL" *(Narr)*.

D'Israeli added "it is said" that the woman was put to death, and that some copies of the edition "have been bought up at enormous prices."

More Motives for Misprints

Here is an odd case in which officialdom may have deliberately misspelled a word for policy purposes. I have two letters on that topic.

From Alan C. Tindal, Longmeadow, Massachusetts—"The top line of the identification card issued to newly commissioned officers during World War II read: 'NOT A PASS. FOR INDENTIFICATION ONLY.' I don't know the true explanation, but the prevailing wisdom at the time was that the misprint was done on purpose. Supposedly, anyone flashing a card with proper spelling would be suspect."

From Mary Louise Gilman, Hanover, Massachusetts—"The letter from Alan C. Tindal on the INdentification card took me back to 1949 in Yokohama and my work as a court reporter for the Department of the Army during the U.S. Occupation of Japan. Military ID cards all read INdentification. What's more, many of our GI's and officers, apparently assuming the Army spelling to be sacrosanct, *pronounced* the redundant N. (The word often came up in the courts-martial I worked on.) *Stars & Stripes* published a letter I wrote on the subject, but I can't say it did much good."

Another interesting class of misprints needs to be mentioned—those that are not consciously intentional but are not purely accidental either. They spring from a person's mental tendencies. Sigmund Freud was fascinated by these psychologically motivated errors. Indeed, he was inclined to see meaning in errors of all kinds, including slips of the tongue, writing mistakes, and inability to remember a name. In general he saw them not as accidents but as serious mental acts. (This concept led to our familiar phrase "Freudian slip.")

As for misprints, Freud saw nothing to prevent our treating them as writing mistakes on the compositor's part and regarding them as being in a very great measure psychologically motivated. In his book *The Psychopathology of Everyday Life*, Freud gave the following as an example of a tendentious, psychologically motivated misprint.

During the rearrangement of Central Europe in 1920 a printed circular said (according to Freud, as translated into English) that Silesia and Teschen had been "divided into two parts, of which one *zuviel* to Poland and the other to Czechoslovakia." This apparently was a shocking misprint. An editor's footnote explained that *zuviel* means "too much," and that the word should have been the similarly pronounced *zufiel,* which means "fell to the share of." The firm that printed the circular was in Teschen and, according to the editor's footnote, "the German-Austrian compositor objected to the distribution of what had been part of the Hapsburg Empire."

That leaves me unsure whether the compositor made the error consciously or did it unintentionally because of his bias. The same uncertainty exists for many other typos. I have no doubt that typesetters make Freudian slips, but I cannot see that most misprints are of that kind. Surely some misprints are simply random accidents, as when a finger hits a wrong key—perhaps the key next door to the right key, or any old wrong key. Some are typesetters' jokes, which may or may not be due to biases. Some blunders are committed by well-intentioned people who think they are correcting an error but change it for the worse. Possibly a psychotherapist could discover in all those cases psychological motives that aren't apparent to an ordinary observer.

The Devil Made Me Do It

Someone believing in satanic power might well think that the Prince of Darkness was at work among the biblical printers of long ago, polluting the holy book with Misprints of Darkness. And indeed, more than one person has pretended to see signs in the composing rooms of the world that something inhuman had passed that way.

Isaac D'Israeli, mentioned earlier, told of such a case. He said that "in the year 1561, was printed a work, entitled the Anatomy of the Mass," which had 172 pages and was "accompanied by an *Errata* of 15 pages!" The editor, a "pious monk," introduced the *Errata* with a claim that the "numerous blunders, never yet equalled in so small a work," were the doings of the Devil, who had obliged the printers to commit them.

Powerful support for the pious monk arose four centuries later in the person of Eli Cantor, owner of a New York typesetting firm and at one time board chairman of Printing Industries of America—also a lawyer, novelist, and playwright. He wrote a small book entitled *The Devil's Pi,* which he called the only true history of printing ever published. He distributed this as a typographic keepsake in 1941 and again in 1967. ("Pi" is a printer's term for type that is spilled or mixed.)

Mr. Cantor, in his history, tells of a time when "Satan and his host were bored in hell." Tempting men into sin was no longer a source of amusement—"men yielded too readily." The imps and demons were "restless with pent-up sulphurous energy." Satan discussed the sad situation with Beelzebub and finally cried out triumphantly that he would invent such a monstrous new mischief that hell would "never again have a dull moment."

"What is this new invention?" Beelzebub asked.

The Devil chuckled and told him to go to the earth and find a man named Johann Gutenberg!

The infernal host heard him and whooped with joy. Gutenberg! "The name growled out of the crevices of the earth, bubbled from the craters of volcanoes, seeped up from the abyss of hell to whisper over the earth the advent of the greatest mischief since man himself was created."

After Satan had caused printing to be invented, he called a vast conclave of cackling, hissing, howling, caterwauling, and cheering demons. He explained the new invention, instructed them on how to abuse it, and sent armies out to printshops everywhere. Eli Cantor, having told all this, described in detail some of the typographical results.

After *Harvard Magazine* published my article on misprints in 1993, Cantor, by then living in Sarasota, Florida, sent a copy of *The Devil's Pi* to the editors with "the thought that it may ease your embarrassment over misprints" by placing the blame "where it properly belongs."

Chapter 7

Benjamin Franklin's Er ata

It is well known that Benjamin Franklin, in his autobiography, confessed several youthful offenses against morality, which he called his "errata." Being a printer, he also committed some errata of a typographical kind. And being a mischievous soul, he loved to tell about misprints and even sometimes to commit them for the fun of it.

During Franklin's early years in Philadelphia, he worked for an eccentric printer named Samuel Keimer. Later, when Franklin was twenty-three, he and a partner bought a dull weekly paper from Keimer and shortened its name to *The Pennsylvania Gazette*. The whole management of the business lay upon Franklin, according to his autobiography.

The first issue came out October 2, 1729, and the paper caught on quickly. For one thing, Philadelphians must have enjoyed Franklin's sprightly news items, some of them more fiction than news. One of the *Gazette's* most entertaining items was amusing because it contained a whopping misprint, and I am far from certain that the misprint was accidental.

The Massachusetts Assembly had sent a rich merchant named Jonathan Belcher to London to argue against paying Governor William Burnet the salary that Burnet had been instructed to demand. In the midst of this effort, word arrived that Burnet had died unexpectedly in America. Belcher got busy and obtained the governorship for himself. On March 5, 1730, Franklin's paper reported the appointment. The story said that Belcher "had the Honour to Kiss his Majesty's Hand," after which Belcher and some gentlemen trading with New England "died elegantly at Pontack's."

Pontack's was a place for elegant *dining.* Presumably Franklin's readers in Philadelphia, or most of them, recognized "died" as a misprint and laughed all over town. The ambitious young printer kept them laughing. In the next issue (March 13) he used the episode as a pretext to describe some shocking typographical errors of the past. The piece, headed *Printerum est errare,* appears as a letter signed "J. T.," but Benjamin's fingerprints are on every line.

He told about the infamous Bible that said "Thou shalt commit adultery." He also reported another biblical misprint (date not given) in the verse that says "I will praise thee; for I am fearfully and wonderfully made" (Psalms 139:14). Franklin said the "e" was dropped from "made," making it "I am fearfully and wonderfully mad." The *Gazette's* readers, no doubt suitably enthralled, were told that this "occasion'd an ignorant Preacher, who took that Text, to harangue his Audience for half an hour on the Subject of *Spiritual Madness.*"

The letter in the *Gazette* also tells of an error in the funeral service of *The Book of Common Prayer* (date not given). The passage "We shall all be changed in a moment, in the twinkling of an eye" (quoted in the prayer book from 1 Corinthians 15:51–52) was said to have been printed without the "c" in "changed," thus rendering it "We shall all be hanged in a moment."

Twenty years later Franklin, writing as Richard Saunders, repeated this story in the preface to the 1750 edition of his almanac, which was then called *Poor Richard improved.* This time he caused Saunders to say he had "heard" that the switch from "changed" to "hanged" had appeared in one edition of the prayer book "to the no small Surprize of the first Congregation it was read to."

In that same 1750 preface Franklin apologized for several errors in his almanac of the year before. Remarkably, one of these was the dropping of the "e" from "made"—the same omission he had earlier mentioned as a humorous biblical misprint. This time there was no doubt that "made" really became "mad" in print. The 1749 almanac has this couplet:

> Learn, wretches, learn the motions of the mind,
> Why you were mad, for what you were design'd, ...

I do not know whether that misprint was engineered by Franklin or another typesetter (by 1750 he was immersed in electrical experiments), but I imagine that he at least read the proof.

Forty more years passed, and "We shall all be hanged" broke out again. The great man died in April 1790. Three months later *The American Museum,* a magazine published in Philadelphia, printed the following item, which I quote in full:

> *Professional anecdote of dr. Franklin*
> When he came to Philadelphia in 1723, he was first employed by one Keimer, a printer,—a visionary whose mind was frequently elevated above the little concerns of life, and consequently very subject to mistakes, which he seldom took the pains to correct. Franklin had frequently reasoned with him upon the importance of accuracy in his profession, but in vain. His fertile head however soon furnished him with an opportunity to second his arguments by proof. They soon after undertook the impression of a primer, which had been lately published in New-England. Franklin overlooked the piece; and when his master had set the following couplet—

When the last trumpet soundeth,
  We shall not all die:
But we shall all be *changed*
  In the twinkling of an eye,

he privately removed the letter *c,* and it was
printed off—

When the last trumpet soundeth,
  We shall not all die:
But we shall all be *hanged*
  In the twinkling of an eye.

The publisher of *The American Museum* was Mathew Carey.
He had worked for Franklin in France, had founded the
magazine in 1787 with Franklin's encouragement, and had
published a number of Franklin's writings. Carey may well
have heard this anecdote from Franklin, perhaps some years
before. Anecdotes are suspect, even when related by famous
people, and I do not take for granted that the two men remembered the facts exactly right. Nevertheless the story
doesn't sound impossible. I would guess that if Franklin did
pluck the "c" out of "changed," he made his point with Keimer
by showing him a galley proof containing the error. If so, the
"c" was probably restored before publication.

In any case it seems clear from all the evidence that
America's first important humorist took much delight in
comical typographical irregularities, whether his own or those
of others, and whether accidental or deliberate.

Chapter 8

Double Jeopardy

Another anecdote told at the *Atlanta Constitution* around 1930 illustrates the category of misprints that occur in the correction of other misprints. A reporter was said to have written a story about a battle-scarred veteran. In the first edition the veteran was "battle-scared," but in the second edition he was "bottle-scarred."

I now know that this is an ancient tale, that it probably never happened in the *Constitution,* and that it may never have happened at all. Andrew Szabo has called my attention to almost exactly the same story in a 1924 printing of Joan Riviere's translation of Sigmund Freud's *A General Introduction to Psycho-Analysis*. Where the story originated is not clear.

Also of doubtful origin is an item received in 1993 from a man who quoted a rural journal thus: "We apologize for the reference in last week's edition to Sgt. Jones of the Detective Farce. We meant, of course, Sgt. Jones of the Defective Force." I wrote to this kind reader and asked if he could remember what rural journal printed the item. He replied, "I suspect that the whole story is apocryphal and there is no rural journal—it just sounded better when I told the story. I have known this story for 50 or 60 years, so its origins are dim. Maybe I made it up."

Another such anecdote that I cannot confirm—though it sounds fairly believable—was broadcast by a Boston disk jockey on January 23, 1969. He said Ronald Heath, living in New Delhi, India, complained that the phone book spelled his name "Ronald Heat." In the next edition he was "Ronald Health."

Of course not all misprints made in the course of correcting other misprints are apocryphal. Almost everybody engaged in printing or publishing can attest that some are authentic. Back when printing was done with metal type, these "double jeopardy" typos used to happen in the following way. A proofreader would mark an error on the galley proof, and a linotype operator would set a new line, which then would be substituted for a perfectly innocent line that happened to begin with the same word as the misprinted line! Another reason corrected passages sometimes contain new mistakes is that the corrections are often inserted just before press time and therefore may not get the careful proofreading that original passages do.

In 1954, when Harvard University Press published *A New Greek Reader*, an errata slip was bound into the book, but several errors were then discovered in the errata slip and it had to be reprinted and substituted.

The word *errata* is the plural of *erratum*, but it's also used in the singular to mean a list of errors. In colonial Philadelphia, one Andrew Steuart printed a Latin grammar of 137 pages and followed it with an *Errata* correcting about seventy-five errors. In 1763, Francis Hopkinson, satirist and prominent Philadelphian, anonymously issued a pamphlet entitled *Errata; or, the Art of Printing Incorrectly,* in which he listed 151 "capital blunders" in Steuart's book and said there were also many smaller mistakes.

Hopkinson declared that Steuart's *Errata* was "more incorrect, if possible, than the *Grammar* itself." But he refrained from listing the errata in the *Errata,* saying that if he had to make that sort of examination he would rather "point out those Places where Mr. Steuart has happened to be right, as we imagine they would not take above *two* or *three* Lines." (Soon after this, Steuart moved to North Carolina.)

The darndest *Errata* that I have seen was the one prepared by James Joyce after his *Finnegans Wake* came out in 1939. The London publisher Faber & Faber issued Joyce's list in 1945—after his death——in the form of a booklet with the title "Correction of Misprints in Finnegans Wake, As Prepared by the Author after Publication of the First Edition." He listed 866 misprints.

Anyone who has looked at *Finnegans Wake* would be inclined to sympathize with the printers, for it contains sentences like this one on page three: "The great fall of the offwall entailed at such short notice the pftjschute of Finnegan, erse solid man, that the humptyhillhead of humself prumptly sends an unquiring one well to the west in quest of his tumptytumtoes." But, amazingly, that passage and most others like it (even the word with one hundred letters on that same page) went uncorrected in the misprints booklet. Apparently they were the way Joyce wanted them, and the printers (no doubt with help from the proofreaders) had somehow managed to get them right. His 866 corrections were mainly things of a different sort. He inserted commas, substituted exclamation points for periods, and removed periods after "Mr." and "Mrs."—all of these in vast numbers.

A couple of misprints in the works of two other Irish writers, Seamus Heaney and W. B. Yeats, were so plausible that they became accepted as authentic—for a while at least.

Seamus Heaney told me about a temporarily acceptable misprint in his poem "At Ardboe Point," which was first published in his book *Door into the Dark* (1969). There is a passage

in the poem about a motorcar encountering a "smoke of flies."
Heaney's manuscript said they "come smattering daintily
against the windscreen." In reading the proof, he noticed
that the printer had made it "shattering." He liked this and
let it stand. But in 1980 when the poem was reprinted in his
Selected Poems, 1965–1975, he changed his mind and went back
to "smattering."

W. B. Yeats, in his poem "Among School Children," mentioned Plato and then "solider Aristotle," but the printer made
it "soldier Aristotle." That version went unchanged in several
printings of Yeats's complete poems while he was still alive,
suggesting that he may have decided he could live with "soldier." In the edition of 1947, eight years after his death,
"solider Aristotle" was substituted.

It's possible that Yeats just didn't notice "soldier" during
all the years when it seemed to be authentic. When his poem
"The Dolls" was published in 1914, the word "bawls" in the
third line came out "balls." This apparently went unnoticed,
because it happened again in 1916 and was not corrected
until later printings.

Chapter 9

"Pub^lic" and Other
Vulnerable Words

Some words are more prone to misprinting than others, and some of the most prone are those that can easily become other correctly spelled words. "Expect" can easily become "except" (and vice versa); "from" can become "form"; "principal" can become "principle"; "smattering" can become "shattering" (as in the preceding chapter); and "naval" can become "navel" (as in Chapter 2). Errors of that sort cannot be detected by the spelling-check systems in computers. Moreover, after they are in type, proofreaders are more apt to miss them than to miss conspicuous garbles. Proofreaders are on the lookout for *misspellings* and are a little less apt to spot a word that is rightly spelled, even if it's the wrong word. Following is a catalog of some of the words that I have seen transformed into similar words—with interesting results.

Public

"Public" is dangerous because its skinny fourth letter has a deplorable tendency to slip out. In some cases (who can say which?) some joker may have consciously aided and abetted the getaway of the "l," just for the laugh. In other cases the typesetter may not have *intended* to set "pubic" but knew that "public" sometimes comes out that way and therefore was *thinking* "pubic" at the time. In still other cases, the omission may have been purely accidental in that the typesetter had never thought of "pubic" in connection with "public." In any case, people reading proof may have failed to notice the omission because a lowercase "l" is not a very noticeable character. Besides, the eye tends to see what the brain *expects* to see. So even a *capital* "L" sometimes manages to escape the word "public" and not be restored.

In 1976 the autobiography of the opera star Beverly Sills, entitled *Bubbles: A Self-Portrait,* came off the press with this remarkable opening sentence: "When I was only three, and still named Belle Miriam Silverman, I sang my first aria in pubic." The horrified publishers rounded up all the copies they could find and issued a second "first edition." But some of the flawed copies survived.

A few years ago the Office of Public Information on the Boston campus of the University of Massachusetts ordered some letterheads. You can guess what happened. The batch came from the printer reading "Office of Pubic Information."

On November 27, 1983, the *Arkansas Gazette,* in Little Rock, ran the following advertisement:

CUSTOMER SERVICE
REPRESENTATIVES
Work immediately until Christmas. Part-time, hours vary.
Must enjoy pubic contact! Call immediately for interview.

In 1984, Thomas K. McCraw's book *Prophets of Regulation,* which eventually won a Pulitzer Prize for history, came out with this index entry: "Pubic Utility Holding Company Act of 1935." McCraw is an excellent proofreader, but he didn't notice the mishap until somebody told him about it much later.

An acquaintance of mine, Debra Ashton, tells me that "public" appeared as "pubic" three times in the first edition of her 1988 book entitled *A Complete Guide to Planned Giving: Everything*

You Need to Know to Compete Successfully for Major Gifts. Nobody noticed the errors until after publication. In the second edition (1991) she corrected two of them and left the third alone for the fun of it—"a secret joke of the author."

And then there is the sad tale of the school dedication in Cambridge, Massachusetts, on October 15, 1983. The city had renovated an old school and renamed it The Graham and Parks Alternative Public School, thereby honoring Saundra Graham, a local political leader, and Rosa Parks, famous for refusing to move to the back of a bus in Montgomery, Alabama, in 1955. A few days before the dedication ceremony, Rosa Parks accepted an invitation to attend, thus ensuring national media coverage.

It was obvious that the old name of the building, Webster Elementary School, carved in stone, could not be replaced in time for the event. Albert Giroux, who was then the public relations director of the school system, told me what happened. He hired a sign-maker to do a rush job, a cloth banner thirty feet long that would cover up the old name. The night before the ceremony, Giroux took the new sign home, unfolded it on his living room floor, and beheld the following in gold capitals sewn on a green background:

THE GRAHAM AND PARKS ALTERNATIVE PUBIC SCHOOL

Almost before Giroux recovered his breath he telephoned the sign-maker. The sign-maker worked all night correcting the error, and the sign was installed in time for the dedication. Giroux tried to keep the near disaster a secret. The principal of the school, however, couldn't resist telling the large crowd of spectators what the sign almost said. So there was a lot of joking in Cambridge about "the grammar school that couldn't spell."

Other Words Containing "l"

The unstable nature of the letter "l" is further demonstrated in this contribution from Angus Thuermer, a journalist of Middleburg, Virginia: "Our Yalie daughter Kitty had just taken the business card of a colleague. 'My goodness,' she said, 'that is certainly an unusual way to spell *William*—with only one "l."' The guy looked at her, reached for his card, looked at it, and said, 'Omigod, I've distributed three thousand of those and this is the first time I've seen it, or anyone has noticed it.'"

The escape of an "l" from a Russian word of twenty-one characters had a tragic result. So said John J. Stephan, historian, who wrote from Honolulu as follows: "To Hall's collection of misprints might be added a new category: fatal. Soviet editors and printers understandably paid particular attention to all references to Stalin. Yet the misprint gremlin cropped up during World War II in the newspaper *Bolshevik Zaporozh'ia* when omission of the letter 'l' traduced *Glavnokomanduiushchii* (Generalissimo) into *Gavnokomanduiushchii* (Turd Commander). The paper's editor shot himself."

Recital

The tiny letter "i" can be elusive too. See what happens when it falls out of "recital." According to physicist Ernest H. Henninger of Greencastle, Indiana, "DePauw University's Performing Arts Center boasts three performance halls, one of which is named Recital Hall. When the hall was built, an identifying plaque was mounted. It was nearly a week before the administration was alerted to the fact that the plaque read 'Rectal Hall.'"

Window

The obituary of a prominent businessman in Troy, New York, describing his upstairs study, is said to have contained this sentence: "He was entertained over the years by three large widows facing the sun."

Deanery

When Louis Lyons was Curator of the Nieman Fellows at Harvard, he remembered a mishap in a telegraphed report when he was covering the presidential campaign of John W. Davis for the *Boston Globe* in 1924. "The candidate was staying at a picturesquely old-fashioned inn. My copy described it as something between a first-class hotel and a *deanery*. But in the printed story it became a *beanery*, an institution evidently more familiar to the telegraph operator."

Intestate

The following statement is found in a 1991 paperback edition of *Straight*, by Dick Francis, page 26: "He had been persuaded by the lawyers not to go interstate." (As if the lawyers were worried about the traffic on I-95.)

Cryptogam

Scientific terms are apt to be risky. One of the riskiest is "cryptogam." Cryptogams, a group of organisms including ferns, mosses, algae, and fungi, are liable to show up as "cryptograms," a word more familiar to typesetters and proofreaders. This happened in the 1988 paperback edition of A. Hunter Dupree's *Asa Gray* (page viii), to the author's regret, though not to his surprise.

Coquilles

The French word *coquilles* means shells, and it also means typographical errors. *Couilles,* without the *q,* is slang for testicles and is used the way "balls" is used in English. So *coquilles* has sometimes become *couilles* in French printshops, just as "public" has become "pubic" where typesetting has been done in English.

My first acquaintance with the two French words came in a letter from Cynthia L. T. Levin, of Washington, D.C., who thought she remembered Jean-Paul Sartre's having used them on a book cover. Her letter was printed in *Harvard Magazine.* Another reader, Alan R. Kabat, saw it and sent it to a friend in Paris, Jean-Pierre Rocroi, who did some research and found, in a 1957 book, a *coquille-couille* anecdote that had nothing to do with Sartre.

According to this yarn a publisher decided to issue a serious book on several topics. The title was *Les Coquilles* (The Misprints) after the first topic. The publisher was determined to have absolutely no misprints in this book, and the most elaborate proofreading precautions were taken. When it was too late to make any changes he looked at the title page and fell stone dead. The "q" had been left out of *Coquilles.*

Meanwhile David Littlejohn, of Berkeley, California, found a *Coquille* anecdote in André Gide's *Journal.* Gide began his journal entry of December 15, 1937, by complaining about an overzealous proofreader who, in the belief that he was correcting an error, had completely altered the meaning of a passage Gide had quoted from Denis Diderot. Then Gide (in the translation provided by Littlejohn) told the following story about one J.-H. Rosny:

> It is related that Rosny, exasperated by the typographical errors that the printers made or let slip by, wrote a vengeful article entitled "Mes Coquilles." When he opened his newspaper the next day, he read with stupefaction, in heavy type, this odd title: "MES COUILLES." A negligent or malicious printer had let the "q" drop out. I am writing this to console myself.

Soi (Oneself)

The English philosopher Herbert Spencer (1820–1903), in his autobiography, said Louis Blanc told him about a typographical blunder in the closing sentence of a story by a French novelist who wrote as La Comtesse ———. As it left her pen (according to Spencer) the sentence said, *"Bien connaître l'amour il faut sortir de soi"* —that is "To know love it is necessary to get out of oneself." But the printers made it *"Bien connaître l'amour il faut sortir le soir"*—"To know love it is necessary to go out in the evening."

Verification

Herbert Spencer also told of a misprint in the early proofs of his book *First Principles.* Said he: "Where I had written—'the daily verification of scientific predictions,' the compositor had put—'the daily versification of scientific predictions.'"

Rabbit

After my misprints article appeared in *Harvard Magazine,* Julius Novick, of New York City, wrote as follows:

Hall brought to mind the assiduous gremlins who used to scatter misprints through *The Village Voice* during my years as a theater critic there. In particular, I remember a felicitous sin of omission, and an equally felicitous sin of commission, committed by the gremlins against my own copy. By doing away with a final "t," they had me declaring, apropos of a revival of Mary Chase's comedy-fantasy *Harvey,* that the hero was accompanied everywhere by "an invisible six-foot-tall white rabbi." (Since *rabbi* can mean "teacher" or "mentor," this was not an entirely inappropriate description of the relationship in the play between the invisible Harvey and his friend Elwood P. Dowd.) Then, not too many weeks later, by the well-placed addition of an "r," the gremlins made me the father of a new word that I still think could be highly pertinent in a number of contexts: *platiturde.*

Whispers

Chess experts insist on silence during their matches. In 1972 when Bobby Fischer and Boris Spassky were battling for the world championship, the *New York Times* said: "Fischer has been known to object to whiskers in the playing room."

Wire

An Apollo moon flight in 1972 was delayed by several problems. A newspaper quoted the flight director: "Perhaps it was a loose wife."

Some Other Vulnerable Words

This recital (watch that "i") could go on and on, but I shall abbreviate the list by simply attesting that I have in my possession clippings or letters showing that:

- ☞ *calm* was printed as *clam.*
- ☞ *food* shortage became *good* shortage.
- ☞ *spry* became *spy* (the victim of this misprint was a spry sixty-three-year-old authority on fossil bats).
- ☞ American *Dental* Association became American *Rental* Association.
- ☞ *did* extremely well became *died* extremely well.
- ☞ *protest* the R.O.T.C. became *protect* the R.O.T.C.
- ☞ her *role* became her *hole.*
- ☞ five *days* a week became five *lays* a week.
- ☞ *take* action became *fake* action.
- ☞ *moral* gadfly became *oral* gadfly.
- ☞ *light* sentences became *life* sentences (this story said a group of women prisoners serving "life sentences" would be housed at the Y.W.C.A. in New Haven, Connecticut).
- ☞ go *east* became go *fast.*
- ☞ *few* became *new.*
- ☞ respected *columnists* became respected *Communists.*

- *friction* became *fiction.*
- Protestant *ethic* became Protestant *ethnic.*
- one of the *winningest* coaches became one of the *sinningest* coaches.
- *conception* became *contraception.*
- she *lives* in the Tampa area became she *lies* in the Tampa area (this was about a woman who underwent nearly two hundred stitches after she was bitten by a barracuda that leaped into a houseboat).
- *shirts, shifts,* and *passing* were altered, not for the better.

One cannot tell which errors mentioned in this chapter were accidental and which were deliberate. Most of those in newspapers happened in the 1960s and 1970s, when the newspaper business was having its serious labor-management troubles and technical difficulties. Whatever the reason, any word that can conveniently get metamorphosed into another word, resulting in a statement that is surprising or comical or deceptive, is a word to beware of. For that matter, unless we are eternally vigilant, any word in the language can strike back at its user.

But the most dangerous word in typography is dangerous not so much for its metamorphosis as for its vanishing act, as you will see in the next chapter.

Chapter 10

The Most D⚛ngerous Word

The most dangerous word is the little word "not." Despite all precautions, typesetters sometimes leave it out and proofreaders sometimes fail to restore it because the sentence *looks* all right without it. When this occurs, the meaning is reversed, the readers are deceived, the author and the publisher go into shock, and chances are somebody is slandered.

Because of these unpleasant consequences, there has long been a common practice in cablegrams—and in copy to be set in type—to follow "not" with "repeat not" in parentheses. And this practice, like the wearing of seat belts, must have prevented many disasters. But more often the word "not" gets no such protection and therefore stands in jeopardy.

The dropping of "not" in old Bibles, including its dropping from "Thou shalt not commit adultery," has already been noted. So has the transformation of "not guilty" to "guilty" in the *Washington Post,* an accident that caused the paper to be sued for libel. Indeed, "not guilty" is one of the most troublesome phrases in the language. Some news organizations fear it so much that they prohibit its use. Instead of "not guilty," reporters must write "innocent."

Here are some more instances of the disappearing "not":

Its disappearance from a 1950 edition of the novel *Washington Square,* by Henry James, had the effect of whitewashing Aunt Lavinia. James had written that she was "not absolutely veracious," but the 1950 version said she was "absolutely veracious."

The *Harvard Crimson* quoted Professor Archibald Cox as saying that "court proceedings will be dropped" against demonstrators who had vacated a university building they had occupied. Cox had really said proceedings will *not* be dropped.

During a controversy over the city manager of Cambridge, Massachusetts, the *Cambridge Chronicle* said that Jonathan Myers, a member of the City Council, "does want a referendum on the city manager." The reporter had accurately written that Myers does *not* want a referendum.

The *Boston Globe* once said that people who feel jittery after drinking only one or two cups of coffee "obviously should drink coffee any time." You can guess what the reporter had actually written.

An editorial in the *Boston Globe* had a sentence that began, "When Mr. Sloan said he would perjure himself." In a later editorial the paper explained that Mr. Sloan had actually said the opposite, but "the word 'not' somehow was dropped from the sentence." (I have the clipping but have lost the date.)

Oddly, "not" is sometimes *inserted* into stories rather than omitted. When the New American Library published a paperback edition of Ayn Rand's *For the New Intellectual* in 1963, the text contained a passage that must have puzzled readers and infuriated the author: "It is philosophy that has brought men to this state—it is not philosophy that can lead them out." Actually she had written "it is *only* philosophy that can lead them out." The publisher bought advertising space to apologize for this "grievous typographical error."

The prefix "non" is vulnerable too, and so are "no" and "now."

"Non" showed up uninvited and unwanted in Sidney Hook's review of the hardcover edition of the book just named, *For the New Intellectual,* by Ayn Rand. His article, as printed by the *New York Times Book Review,* contained this passage: "non-consistency is never sufficient condition of truth." A correction April 23, 1961, said "non-consistency" should have been "consistency."

"No" can vanish like "not," and presumably it vanished from this sentence about the death of a ten-year-old boy: "They [the police] said there were marks of violence on his body and that the death 'did not look suspicious.'"

"Now" is a risky word simply because it looks like "no" and "not."

At the Harvard commencement of June 12, 1969, President Nathan Pusey allowed a representative of the Students for a Democratic Society to speak. The *Boston Globe,* however, confused the issue by quoting Pusey this way: "We will not let the representative of SDS say his piece." The word "not" should have been "now."

When the *New York Times* reported allegations that agents of the South Korean government had murdered a journalist, the paper added that "now proof" of the charge had come to light. The next day the paper corrected this to "no proof."

Later the *Times,* erring in the opposite direction, said racial stereotypes in Louisville were "not moderating." The next day the paper said the phrase should have been "now moderating."

Therein is a lesson for writers. When using "now," they should consider placing the word, if possible, where it is unlikely to emerge as "not." For example, "Stereotypes now are moderating" is safer than "Stereotypes are now moderating."

Chapter 11

Mailing Lists, Advertisements, and Stone Tablets

Misprints are ubiquitous. They violate mailing lists, advertisements, telephone books, menus, book indexes, tombstones, automobile license plates, baseball bats, commercial signs, bank statements, diplomas, crossword puzzles, play-by-play reports of chess matches, and indeed probably every graphic form of expression in which words and numbers are employed.

Mailing Lists

Misprints often occur in mailing lists, as everybody knows. And when a misprint occurs in one mailing list, it's apt to spread to others.

Toward the end of 1990 I received a solicitation from the American Diabetes Association addressed not to Max R. Hall but to "Max R. Ahll." During the next three years this new person, "Max R. Ahll," received appeals from thirty-one other organizations, including Mothers Against Drunk Driving, Action on Smoking and Health, the League of Women Voters, Station WGBH (Boston), the Special Olympics, the New England Home for Little Wanderers, and organizations concerned with Alzheimer's, arthritis, cancer, epilepsy and heart disease. (See list headed "The Traveling Misprint," p. 58.)

Some of the organizations sent clumps of "Mr. Max R. Ahll" labels to be stuck on outgoing mail. Mothers Against Drunk Driving equipped Max R. Ahll with an identification card. Sometimes Hall and Ahll received solicitations from the same outfit on the same day.

As more and more appeals to Ahll arrived in my mailbox, I showed them to friends and family for their amusement. One day I received a letter signed Ycnan Ahll. It said:

Dear Mr. Ahll,

I am writing you because I believe we may be related. I came across your name on a mailing list and couldn't believe my eyes. My father was of Arabic descent; I was told his grandfather used the "AL-" before his name and dropped the hyphen at some point. I grew up on a Navajo reservation—my Arabic-German parents having chosen the Indian way of life and culture. I have never come across our last name except for a cousin in N.Y.C. I would like to learn more of your ancestors.

Sincerely,
Ycnan Ahll

This had me fooled—and I was about to answer it—until I noticed that "Ycnan" is "Nancy" spelled backward. Nancy is one of my daughters.

Advertisements

Mix-ups in ads can be especially grievous, forcing advertisers to make anxious explanations about prices and products.

Continental Airlines, after running an ad in the *Boston Herald*, took out new ads declaring in large type: YOU WEREN'T THE ONLY ONES SURPRISED TO SEE A $48 FARE TO L.A.! (People who bought their $48 tickets on the day the ad appeared were allowed to use them.)

Here is an advertising misprint that happened more than two centuries ago. A farm near Philadelphia was advertised in the *Pennsylvania Packet.* The ad said the farm was situated "so high that none of the injurious frogs from the Schuylkill reach it." The word, of course, should have been "fogs."

In the fall of 1975, when the *Harvard Business Review* advertised for an assistant editor, one of the stated duties was "understanding the managing editor." Presumably the word should have been "understudying." The misprint went uncorrected in the *Harvard University Gazette* week after week.

In 1984 the town of Greenfield, Massachusetts, advertised for a meter maid at an hourly wage of $15.18, a misprint for $5.18. "I was the first to apply for the job," said the police chief. He said at least forty-five applications came in during the first twenty-four hours, including one from a meter maid already on duty.

In a periodical called *Africa Report* (May 1971), Harvard University Press advertised a book with the surprising title *Muslim Brotherhoods and Politics in Israel.* Its real title was *Muslim Brotherhoods and Politics in Senegal.* The Press never found out how this error occurred.

Telephone Books

The following is the biggest phone book error that has come my way. In 1982, British Telecom issued its new edition for the West Thames area. All names beginning with E and F were left out, and those beginning with G and H were printed twice.

Menu Misprints

Menu misprints are easy to find—just eat out. One example will be enough here. The printed menu at a U.S. noncommissioned officers' club in Okinawa in the early 1960s offered this delicacy, month after month: "Bowel of chili."

Indexes

An index entry containing "pubic" instead of "public" was described earlier. Here is a startling index entry from the bulky 1959 edition of *Textbook of Pediatrics,* edited by Waldo E. Nelson: "Birds, for the, 1–1413." This was not a printer's error, for somebody who helped make the lengthy index (said to be a family member) inserted it as a joke. I include it here because it shows the kind of thing a proofreader can miss while looking for misspellings.

Things Sewn

A "public/pubic" error in a 30-foot banner sewn for a school dedication was mentioned in Chapter 9. A somewhat similar mishap, but without the "pubic," happened on the Lowell campus of the University of Massachusetts when the governor was there in 1991 to sign an education bill. A large banner prepared for the occasion spelled the name of the state MASSASSACHUSETTS. It was said to have been taken down shortly before the ceremony.

Another sewing "misprint" in my collection is in a sampler stitched in 1812 by Lydia Brown, a fourteen-year-old schoolgirl in a town called Nine Partners, New York. The sampler has four alphabets, lacking only one letter among them, and a couplet with one misspelling: "The needle and the pen impart / Instuction to the youthful heart."

Nicknames

When my friend Randolph Fort was appointed Beauty Editor of the Emory University yearbook in the early 1930s, a misprinted headline in the *Emory Wheel* made him the "Betuty Editor." For the rest of his life his friends called him "Betuty."

Plaques and Things Carved in Stone

Errors in newspapers are to be expected, what with the speed of publication, but how do you explain errors on big solid objects?

For example, on opening day of the 1969 baseball season, when President Nixon threw out the first ball, his Presidential Seal of Office stared blandly from the front of the grandstand with "President" spelled "Presidnt."

When *PC Magazine,* a publication about personal computers, picked the top products of the year 1988, the winners received plaques labeled *FIFTH ANNUAL AWARDS FOR TECHNICHAL EXCELLENCE.*

And finally, consider the case of the handsome carved tablet in the arcade of Harvard's Holyoke Center, honoring Edward W. Forbes for services to the University. It had a spelling error—*AQUISITION* for *ACQUISITION*—that was not caught until after the huge slab of slate had been affixed high on the arcade wall in 1966. The building's architect had approved a sketch containing the error. The stone carvers corrected it without removing the tablet, and the "erasure" is almost invisible, but it took them about four days to grind down the surface and recarve part of the inscription.

When such a thing can happen in a carved tribute to a distinguished alumnus in the bosom of a university, it can happen in any newspaper, magazine, book, or stone tablet anywhere, any time.

The Traveling Misprint

Organizations addressing mail
to the nonexistent Max R. Ahll (see pp. 53–54)

Action on Smoking and Health
Alzheimer's Disease and Related Disorders
  Association (Chicago)
Alzheimer's Disease Research (Rockville, Maryland)
American Cancer Society
American Diabetes Association
American Heart Association
American Parkinson Disease Association
American Red Cross
Arthritis Foundation
Boston Food Bank
Catholic Relief Services
Covenant House
Dana-Farber Cancer Institute
Epilepsy Foundation of America
Greater Boston Food Bank
Law Enforcement Officers Memorial Fund
League of Women Voters
March of Dimes
Massachusetts Easter Seal Society
Memorial Sloan-Kettering Cancer Center
Mothers Against Drunk Driving (Washington)
Mothers Against Drunk Driving (Irving, Texas)
National Abortion Rights Action League
National Wildlife Federation
New England Home for Little Wanderers
Project Bread
Project Hope
Special Olympics
United States Olympic Committee
Vietnam Veterans Memorial Fund
WGBH, Boston
World Wildlife Fund

Chapter 12

That Typographical Error:
It Will Hap~pen!

The typographical error is a slippery thing and sly,
You can hunt till you are dizzy, but it somehow will get by
    Till the forms are off the presses. It is strange how
        still it sleeps;
    It shrinks down in a corner, and it never stirs or peeps.
That typographical error, too small for human eyes
Till the ink is on the paper, when it grows to mountain size.
    The boss just stares with horror, then he grabs his hair
        and groans;
The copy reader drops his head upon his hands and moans.
The remainder of the issue may be clean as clean can be,
But that typographical error is the only thing you see.
                            —Author unknown

This anonymous poem is from a book by Albert Johannsen, *The House of Beadle and Adams and Its Dime and Nickel Novels: The Story of a Vanished Literature,* Volume 3 (copyright © 1962 by the University of Oklahoma Press) and is reprinted here by permission of the publisher.

The truth of the poem is reinforced by what happened when two periodicals picked it up.

Antiquarian Bookman, reprinting it on November 19, 1962, made an error in the process—an erroneous period after "too small for human eyes."

The Harvard Librarian, a newsletter, reprinting it from *Antiquarian Bookman* in December 1962, repeated the erroneous period and made a new typographical error, printing "The boss just *stars* with horror ..."

Those devilish gremlins get around, and they never sleep.

Notes and Credits

(Many of the descriptions of misprints in the text
are self-sufficient and need no citations here.)

Page

v. "An Embarrassment of Misprints" (the article) reprinted in three
other periodicals. They are:
Scholarly Publishing, October 1993, 11–20.
*The Catchline: Bulletin of the Association of Reporters of Judicial Deci-
sions,* in three installments beginning September 1993.
Catholic Digest, January 1994 (condensed form), 102–107.

1. "Printers have persecuted me." This and other Bibles with faulty
passages are described in *Brewer's Dictionary of Phrase & Fable,* re-
vised and enlarged [1953], 102–104. The Bibles themselves are
extremely hard to find. I am indebted to Anthony W. Shipps, of
the Indiana University Libraries, for steering me to *Brewer's* and
for other advice.

5. "Navel Academy." I first heard of this typo when Mark Carroll sent
me a clipping about it from the *Washington Post* of Dec. 21, 1990.
Later he reprinted my *Harvard Magazine* article in *Scholarly
Publishing* when he was editor of that journal, and still later, as an
editor at Fulcrum Publishing, he encouraged me to expand the
article into a book.

6. "Poofreading." Edward Weeks, *This Trade of Writing* (1935), 192–
193; F. N. Doubleday, *The Memoirs of a Publisher* (1972), 220; Ferris
Greenslet, *Under the Bridge* (1943), 65.

6. "In bed with coed." Chalmers M. Roberts, *The Washington Post: The First 100 Years* (1977), 205–206. Murrey Marder of the *Post* first put me on to this.

7. The 5-year-old truck driver. Jan. 11, 1965. In the Late City Edition he had aged to 25.

7. Luci Baines Johnson. July 3, 1965. In the Late City Edition her birth date was corrected to July 2, 1947.

7. The 3-year-old repairman. Dec. 10, 1965. A different version of the story was used in the Late City Edition, and it omitted his age.

8. The 181-year-old stunt man. Sept. 2, 1977.

8. Tchaikovsky. *Boston Globe* of May 5, 1991. The concert had really taken place May 5, 1881.

9. Libel suit. The *Washington Post* typo occurred Feb. 5, 1976. The libel case was *Donaldson* v. *Washington Post Co.* in D.C. Superior Court, which made its ruling Nov. 22, 1977.

9. "Red-nosed Archbishop." Walter Waggoner, then in the London bureau of the *New York Times,* told about this typo in a letter printed in *Nieman Reports,* April 1961.

10. "Old Eyesore." Grady Clay's letter, *Harvard Magazine,* Sept.–Oct. 1993.

11. Recipe errors. Molly O'Neill, "When Recipe Writers' Worst Nightmares Haunt Their Days," *New York Times,* June 19, 1991.

11. Melville's *White-Jacket.* The "soiled fish" misprint occurred in *The Works of Herman Melville: Standard Edition,* Vol. 6 (1922), 497, and was perpetuated in several later editions. F. O. Matthiessen's discussion is on p. 392 of his *American Renaissance* (1941). Recent printings of the novel make the fish "coiled," as in the original publication of 1850. Apparently the first writer to point out the misprint and Matthiessen's misfortune was John W. Nicol in *American Literature,* November 1949. My first knowledge of the affair came from Fredson Bowers, "The Ecology of American Literary Texts," *Scholarly Publishing,* January 1973.

11. Shakespeare's sonnets. Donald W. Foster, "Master W. H., R.I.P." *PMLA (Publication of the Modern Language Association),* January 1987, 42–54.

12. Shryock and "New Jersey Giants." Whitfield J. Bell, Jr., of Philadelphia, a historian, heard the story from Shryock long ago and wrote me about it in 1993. His letter is in *Harvard Magazine,* Sept.–Oct. 1993.

12. Error in *The Spectator.* In case some reader happens to be interested in the anecdote of the cruel Englishman, see Richard Ligon, *A True & Exact History of the Island of Barbados* (1657); Lawrence Marsden Price, *Inkle and Yarico Album* (1937); and Max Hall, "Hoax upon Hoax; or, Too Many Inventions for Ben," *Emory University Quarterly,* winter 1960.

13. Horticultural/historical. Louis L. Tucker to Fellows of the Library, April 1988. Conversation with Bruce Wilcox, Jan. 6, 1994.

14. "Mr." Ruth Bader Ginsburg. D. Scott Sherrill, a New York lawyer, sent me a facsimile of this mistake with the comment "I'd call this the Harvard typo of the century." His letter is in *Harvard Magazine,* Sept.–Oct. 1993.

14. Zemko and "morals." *Regional Standard* (based in Colchester, Connecticut), Oct. 2, 1993, and Oct. 23, 1993; *Norwich Bulletin,* Oct. 4, 1993. I thank Leeland J. Cole-Chu, a lawyer of New London, Connecticut, for sending me those three clippings.

15. *Journal of Health and Social Behavior.* The typo appeared in September 1985, p. 156. My psychologist daughter, Judith A. Hall, provided a facsimile.

15. Public Broadcasting System. Virginia Kane, of San Clemente, California, first reported this one. Her letter is in *Harvard Magazine,* Mar.–Apr. 1994.

16. Erroneous numbers.
    Stonehenge, *New York Times* early edition, Aug. 19, 1969, p. 49.
    Sulphur oxides, *New York Times,* May 1, 1971; correction May 2.
    World energy, a letter in the *New York Times,* Jan. 19, 1972; correction Jan. 25.
    Saugus incinerator, *Boston Globe,* Apr. 4, 1973; correction Apr. 6.
    Massachusetts governor, *Boston Globe,* Mar. 20, 1981; correction Mar. 21.

17. The Great Auk. "Birds of Yesterday," in *About the Exhibits,* by Elizabeth Hall and Max Hall, 3rd ed. (1985), 11.

18. Madame de Gaulle. *New York Times,* Apr. 27, 1960, in all editions. Correction published Apr. 29.

19. Joseph Curran's telegram. The lines were omitted in all editions of the *New York Times,* Oct. 9, 1962. Correction Oct. 17.

19. $120 million in refunds. *New York Times,* June 27, 1969.

19. Luther L. Terry. *New York Times,* Oct. 25, 1972. Though the word "former" was inserted in a late edition, this left readers of the early editions with false information. Dr. Terry may have protested this; at least a correction of the error appeared in the early editions of Oct. 27.

20. Bombing of Cambodia. *New York Times,* July 19, 1973; correction July 20.

20. "Burned down Harvard Hall." *An Introduction to Harvard* (1948), 2.

20. Dr. Krumbhaar's embarrassment. *Harvard College Class of 1904: Fiftieth Anniversary Report,* 265; *Supplementary Report, 50th Anniversary Reunion,* 51.

22. Bret Harte anecdote. I first saw this in the *Brown Alumni Monthly* of April 1961, which said it came from Warren L. Carleen. I wrote to him, but he didn't remember where he got it. Meanwhile Anthony Shipps sent me a slightly different version he had spotted in Robert Hendrickson's *American Literary Anecdotes* (1990), 100. I wrote to Hendrickson and asked where he found the story, but never got a reply.

22. The "To-remain Bible." *Brewer's,* 104, says the mistake was repeated in Bibles published in 1805 and 1819.

23. Two Harlow Shapley stories. Joseph F. Dolan's letter to me was adapted by *Harvard Magazine* and published in its issue of Nov.–Dec. 1993.

25. "Wicked Bible" no accident. P. M. Handover, *Printing in London* (1960), 84–85.

27. "Unrighteous Bible" and other misprinted Bibles. *Brewer's,* 103–104.

28. Adam and Eve and the printer's widow. Isaac D'Israeli, *Curiosities of Literature,* 7th ed., Vol. 1 (1823), 148.

28. "Indentification card." The Tindal letter is in *Harvard Magazine,* Sept.–Oct. 1993.

29. Sigmund Freud. For his views on errors see his *A General Introduction to Psycho-Analysis,* translated by Joan Riviere (I consulted the 1963 edition of her 1920 translation), especially 41, 54; and his *The Psychopathology of Everyday Life* (1960 translation by Alan Tyson, edited by James Strachey), especially 129–131. The *zuviel* misprint is described on 130–131. I am grateful to Andrew Szabo, of Hoboken, New Jersey, for getting me interested in Freud's psychology of errors.

30. "Anatomy of the Mass." *Curiosities of Literature* (as above), 145–146.

33. "Benjamin Franklin's Errata." This chapter first appeared (in a slightly different form) as an article, "Franklin's Other Errata," in *Franklin Gazette* (published by Friends of Franklin, Philadelphia), summer 1993.

34. Franklin's letter on printers' errors. Reprinted in *The Papers of Benjamin Franklin,* Yale ed., I:169–170.

34. Franklin's 1749 and 1750 almanacs. *Papers,* III:341, 438.

35. *The American Museum* anecdote: July 1790, p. 24.

37. Freud and battle-scarred veteran. The anecdote is repeated in later editions of Freud's book (see his "second lecture"). A footnote by the translator merely says "English example." Apparently she furnished it to illustrate Freud's category of cases in which errors multiply.

39. Yeats misprints. *The Variorum Edition of the Poems of W. B. Yeats,* ed. Peter Allt and Russell K. Alspach (1957), 319, 445.

42. "Sang my first aria in pubic." Letter from John F. Adams, assistant dean of the Harvard Extension School, in *Harvard Magazine,* Sept.–Oct. 1993. He owns one of the flawed copies, and I have acquired another.

42. "Must enjoy pubic contact." Norvell N. Plowman, lawyer of Little Rock, Arkansas, sent in a facsimile of this ad along with other interesting typos. For example, he provided a "business reply" envelope that says "No postage necessary if mauled in the United States."

44. William with one "l." Thuermer's letter is in *Harvard Magazine,* Sept.–Oct. 1993.

44. "A new category: fatal." Stephan's letter is in *Harvard Magazine,* Nov.–Dec. 1993. He cited Vladimir Voinowich, *Anti-sovetskii Sovetskii Soiuz,* 214.

44. "Rectal Hall." Henninger's letter in *Harvard Magazine,* Sept.–Oct. 1993.

44. "Three large widows." Grady Clay's letter in *Harvard Magazine,* Sept.–Oct. 1993.

45. Candidate in a beanery. *Nieman Reports,* January 1961.

45. *Coquilles* and *couilles.* These letters in *Harvard Magazine:* Levin, Nov.–Dec. 1993; Littlejohn, Jan.–Feb. 1994; Rocroi, Mar.–Apr. 1994. The anecdote that Rocroi found is in *Esprit, es-tu là?* by Michel Chrestien (Gallimard, 1957), 76. Chrestien attributed the story to the writer Léon-Paul Fargue.

46. Spencer's two misprint stories. *An Autobiography* by Herbert Spencer (1904), I:535–536, II:71–72. Robert L. Carneiro, Curator of Anthropology in the American Museum of Natural History, put me on to these.

47. *The Village Voice* typos. Novick's letter in *Harvard Magazine,* Nov.–Dec. 1993.

48. "Whiskers in the playing room." July 19, 1972. This was corrected in a later edition of the same date.

48. Apollo and the loose wife. *Boston Globe,* Feb. 6, 1971.

50. Aunt Lavinia. Fredson Bowers, "The Ecology of American Literary Texts," *Scholarly Publishing,* January 1973.

51. Court proceedings not dropped. Mar. 16, 1971; correction Mar. 17.

51. Cambridge city manager. Nov. 25, 1992; correction Dec. 3.

51. Jittery coffee drinkers. Jan. 28, 1970.

51. Ayn Rand on philosophy. Ad in *New York Times Book Review,* paperback book section, Jan. 5, 1964.

52. "Marks of violence." *New York Times,* Jan. 12, 1971, early edition.

52. Korean journalist. Sept. 22, 1975; correction Sept. 23.

52. Louisville stereotypes. Dec. 9, 1975; correction Dec. 10.

54. Air fare of $48. Ad in *Boston Herald,* May 10, 1993; ad in *Boston Globe,* May 17.

55. "Injurious frogs." Letter from Whitfield J. Bell, Jr., in *Harvard Magazine,* Sept.–Oct. 1993. The ad appeared Nov. 15, 1783. Bell commented that maybe the typesetter had seen *Jurassic Park.*

55. "Understanding the managing editor." One of the *Harvard University Gazettes* in which the ad appeared was that of Nov. 14, 1975.

55. The meter maid. Report in *Boston Globe,* Oct. 26, 1984.

55. Telephone book mix-up. Associated Press report in *Sarasota Herald-Tribune,* Feb. 27, 1982.

55. "Bowel of chili." Reported by my son, Clay M. Hall, who was there.

56. "Birds, for the." Letter from Dr. David H. Barnhouse, of Pittsburgh, in *Harvard Magazine,* Nov.–Dec. 1993.

56. Too many ASSes in Massachusetts. Associated Press photo in *Berkshire Eagle,* July 12, 1991.

56. A sewing "misprint" of 1812. Howard Sprague, of Salem, Massachusetts, sent me a photograph of the sampler, which is reproduced in *Harvard Magazine,* Nov.–Dec. 1993, along with his letter, in which he says: "Lydia survived the embarrassment of her youthful error and went on to live a long and useful life." She was his grandmother's great-aunt.

57. "Presidnt" Nixon. Photographs appeared in the press, including the front page of the *New York Times,* Apr. 8, 1969.

57. Awards for "technichal excellence." Photograph of plaque is on the magazine's cover, Jan. 17, 1989. My son-in-law Fred Gordon provided a copy.

57. Tablet honoring Forbes. Interviews with John Benson, the stone carver, and William Bentinck-Smith, who discovered the error in 1966. I first learned about it in 1991 from my son, Clay, who had noticed the error when he was a Harvard student in 1966.

Index